T0353757

These Meditations
of *My Heart*

CHARLES ALONZO FREEMAN

WestBow Press books may be ordered through booksellers or by contacting:

WestBow Press
A Division of Thomas Nelson & Zondervan
1663 Liberty Drive
Bloomington, IN 47403
www.westbowpress.com
844-714-3454

ISBN: 979-8-3850-3995-1 (sc)
ISBN: 979-8-3850-3994-4 (e)

Library of Congress Control Number: 2024926398

Print information available on the last page.

WestBow Press rev. date: 02/11/2025

WESTBOW
PRESS®
A DIVISION OF THOMAS NELSON
& ZONDERVAN

INTRODUCTION

"The Meditations of My Heart" has been designed as a collection of poetic writings. These writings have come in the midst of what I would call the most difficult storm that I have faced in my life. As I began to turn from a life of sin and rebellious living before the God and Creator of the universe, the world became as a frigid iceberg. This time period caused me to turn to my childhood love, writing. A secret love that has always been dear to me, it was at the most adverse of times that the Lord allowed me to enjoy this love in my life.

It is not without caution that I render these meditations. I quote from one of the Old Testament books of prophecy "The heart is deceitful above all things, and desperately wicked; who can know it?" With this verse in mind I pray and will continue to pray that these meditations of my heart are pleasing in the sight of God and that they will be a blessing to all who may journey into them.

Finally, brethren, whatever things are true, whatever things are noble,

whatever things are just, whatever things are pure,

whatever things are lovely, whatever things are of good report,

if there is any virtue and if there is anything praiseworthy—

meditate on these things.

Philippians 4:8

A Free Man

I belong, therefore, I no longer have to belong

I have not need to ponder or sing a sad song

Joyful noises parade from my lips

Back into reality my mind no longer takes trips

A smile has become my favorite attire

Bringing glory and honor to God is my only desire

Here I am the same place I started

With a peace of mind I venture into the unchartered

I'm a free man

But now having been set free from sin,

and having become slaves of God,

you have your fruit to holiness,

and the end, everlasting life.

Romans 6:22

He has a Plan

I was broken and desperate, hopeless and lost

For the first time in my life, I stopped to count the cost

There's no price I could pay…No words I could say

This beautiful gift of life I was slowly giving away

Trapped in sin, trapped by the evil within

I was playing a game… there was no way I could win

I started searching for help, looking for a hand

The thought crossed my mind, God has a perfect plan

My Lord please save me, that was my cry

As I felt my pain easing… I let go a sigh

His grace and His mercy are so beautiful to me

From darkness to light… He allowed me to see

He granted me deliverance… and I became a man

For as long as live I will hold to His hand

Now I have joy and peace in my mind

My God is love… and His will is divine

For we are His workmanship,

created in Christ Jesus for good works,

which God prepared beforehand that we should walk in them.

Ephesians 2:10

Lesson Learned

A lesson of mine comes through one circle in time

I was so blind

It would all be easy if I could just press rewind

No buttons in life, I must deal with trouble and strife

The chances I take are they for profit or just fate

I live and I learn it's so beautiful to watch the world turn

I love to watch it turn I just hope it doesn't cause my soul to burn

Real is real and fake is fake how many times do I get to say it was just a mistake

With a tear in my eye I am not afraid to cry

Shedding a tear is a lot better than living a lie

And you shall know the truth,

and the truth shall make you free.

John 8:32

The Way Up

O Lord, O Lord
am I low enough for thee?

O Lord, O Lord
at your feet .. I wanna be

I wanna be a vessel,
used in your service
the thought of not being low enough
makes me kinda nervous

O Lord, O Lord
I wanna worship thee

Just the thought of your presence
brings me to my knees

At the foot of your throne
O Lord!.... is where I belong

Forever in worship…
until You call me home

And He sat down, called the twelve, and said to them,

"If anyone desires to be first, he shall be last of all and servant of all."

Mark 9:35

God Is Love

Love, love, love God is love

This is something I never knew

Too engulfed with self… and busy being mad at you

A heart constantly filled with rage

So much so… I've been stuck at the same stage

A touch of love… so many acts of grace

Even despite myself… love put me in my place

I no longer block my heart… I saturate it with love

Thank you God for this perfect gift from above

Thank you God… I now know how to love

If someone says, "I love God," and hates his brother,

he is a liar; for he who does not love his brother whom he has seen,

how can he love God whom he has not seen?

1John 4:20

A Permanent Visitor

He came to visit me one night … I was down on a knee

My Lord and My Savior… came to visit me

I never saw Him …or even heard a sound

As I opened up my heart… I felt His presence all around

At first I felt a rush….my heart was beating fast

Overwhelmed by this feeling… I hoped forever it would last

I know He came to visit… this I do know

When I got up from my knee… I felt my spirit glow

My Savior came to visit me…. everything was alright

He gave me the confidence… to trust Him day and night

I'm glad He came to visit … glad I was on His mind

From that very moment… my past was left behind

As far as the east is from the west,

So far has He removed our transgressions from us

Psalm 103:12

19

The Wondrous Cross

When I survey, when I survey the wondrous cross

I find myself oh but lost

A place of refuge, from a focus on me

At the cross my Savior died for me

My sin, my guilt, my shame

My hurt, my pride, my pain

God forbid that I should boast

Save in the cross, Save in the cross

Nothing am I, look to the tree

Tis was there He died for me

Calvary, Calvary thank you my Lord for Calvary

Death is gone, now free from sin

The Holy Spirit is now within

I have been crucified with Christ;

it is no longer I who live, but Christ lives in me;

and the life which I now live in the flesh

I live by faith in the Son of God,

who loved me and gave Himself for me.

Galatians 2:20

It's Okay With Me

Another blessing I don't need

You've already blessed me with the Seed

It crushed the serpent, and delivered my soul

Now I'm free, for your name to extol

It's okay with me today

It's okay now that I know the Way

Suffering you did and suffering you died

Suffering for all my sin to hide

It was the blood that cleansed my soul

It was the blood that gave your name to extol

Blessed be the God and Father of our Lord Jesus Christ,

who has blessed us with every spiritual blessing

in the heavenly places in Christ

Ephesians 1:3

Printed in the United States
by Baker & Taylor Publisher Services